Impressum
Verlag: BABADADA GmbH, Nedderfeld 112 , 22529 Hamburg
Geschäftsführer / Verlagsleitung: Harald Hof
Druck: Books on Demand GmbH, In de Tarpen 42, 22848 Norderstedt

Imprint
Publisher: BABADADA GmbH, Nedderfeld 112 , 22529 Hamburg, Germany
Managing Director / Publishing direction: Harald Hof
Print: Books on Demand GmbH, In de Tarpen 42, 22848 Norderstedt

scol

school

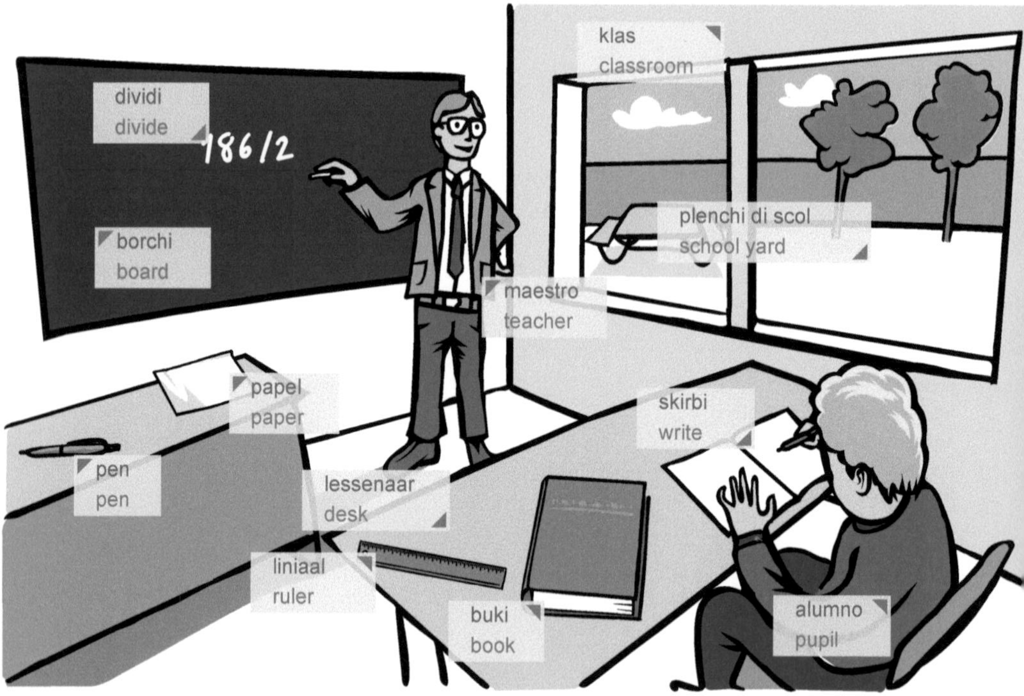
klas
classroom
dividi
divide
186/2
borchi
board
plenchi di scol
school yard
maestro
teacher
papel
paper
skirbi
write
pen
pen
lessenaar
desk
liniaal
ruler
buki
book
alumno
pupil

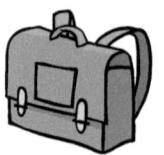

tas di scol

satchel

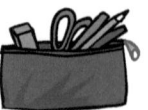

etui

pencil case

potlood

pencil

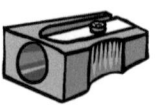

slijper

pencil sharpener

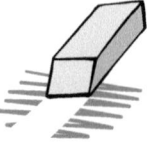

gum

rubber

buki di pinta

drawing pad

pintura

drawing

cuashi

paintbrush

caha di verf

paint box

sker

scissors

lijm

glue

schrift

exercise book

huiswerk

homework

number

number

suma

add

kita

subtract

multiplica

multiply

conta

calculate

letter

letter

alfabet

alphabet

palabra

word

texto

text

lesa

read

krijt

chalk

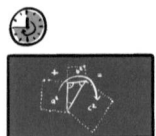

les

lesson

klassenboek

register

examen

exam

diploma

certificate

uniform di scol

school uniform

estudio

education

enciclopedia

encyclopedia

universidad

university

microscop

microscope

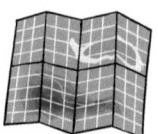

mapa

map

bari di sushi

waste-paper basket

biahamento
travel

hotel
hotel
Grand
posada
hostel
ROOMS
EXCHANGE
oficina di cambio
bureau de change
maleta
suitcase
auto
car

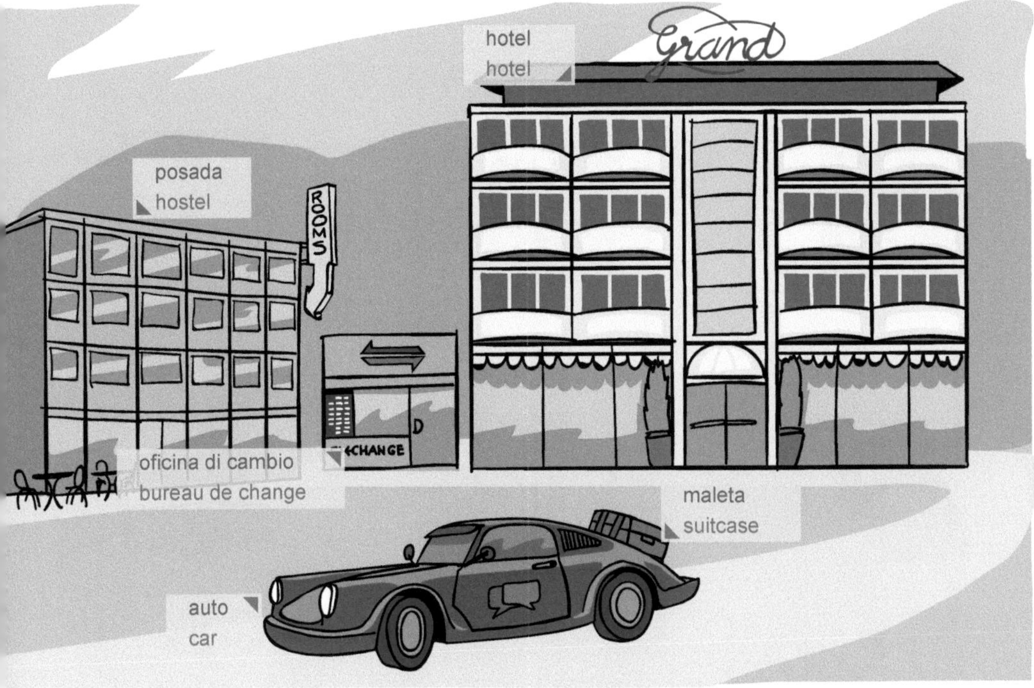

idioma

language

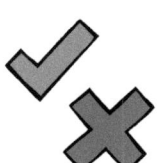

si / no

yes / no

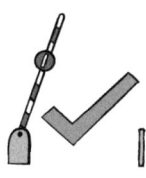

bon

Okay

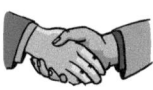

hallo

hello

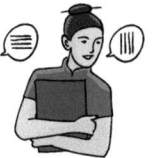

tolk

translator

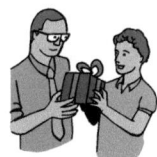

masha danki

Thank you

Cuanto esaki ta costa?

how much is...?

Mi no ta compronde

I do not understand

problema

problem

bon nochi

Good evening!

Bon dia!

Good morning!

Bon nochi!

Good night!

ayo

bye bye

direccion

direction

maleta

luggage

handbag

bag

rugtas

backpack

huesped

guest

camber

room

slaapzak

sleeping bag

tent

tent

informacion pa turista

tourist information

lama

beach

credit card

credit card

desayuno

breakfast

cuminda di merdia

lunch

cuminda di anochi

dinner

carchi

ticket

cabe'i boto

lift

stampia

stamp

grens

border

duana

customs

embahada

embassy

visa

visa

paspoort

passport

transport
transport

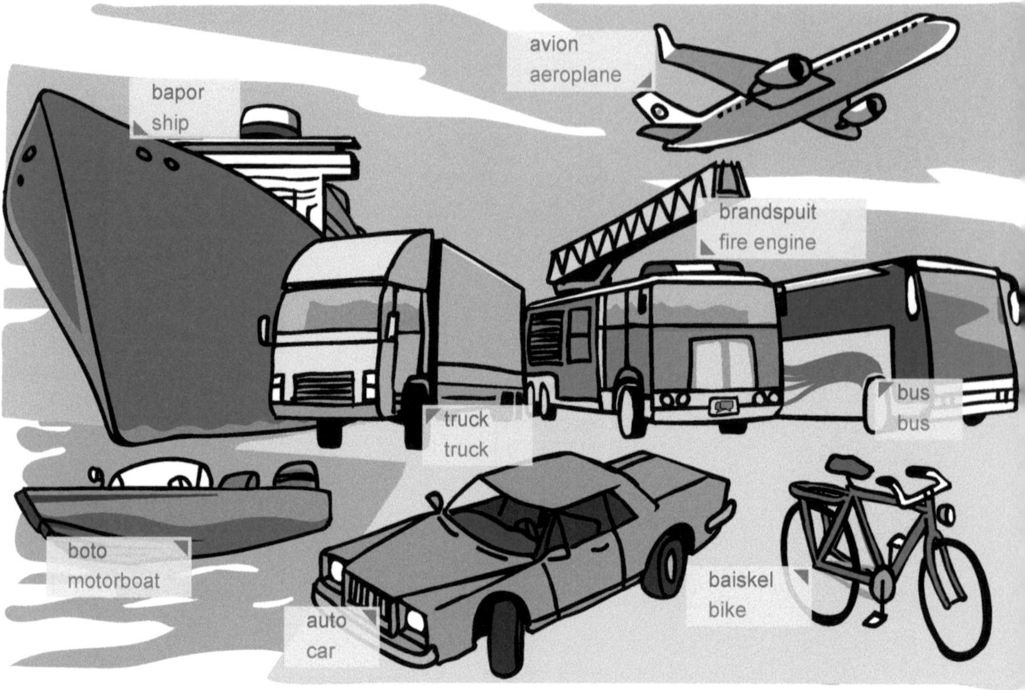
avion
aeroplane
bapor
ship
brandspuit
fire engine
bus
bus
truck
truck
boto
motorboat
baiskel
bike
auto
car

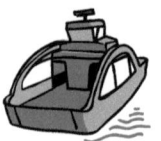

ferry
ferry

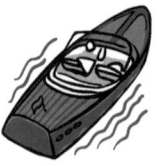

boto
boat

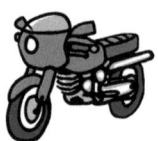

brommer
motorbike

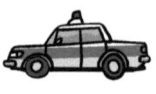

auto di polis
police car

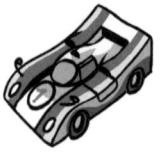

auto di careda
racing car

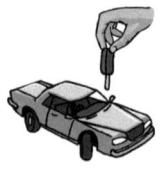

auto di huur
rental car

car sharing
car sharing

takelwagen
breakdown truck

dump truck
refuse truck

motor
motor

gasolin
fuel

pomp di gasolin
petrol station

borchi di trafico
traffic sign

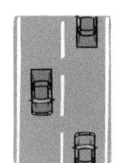

trafico
traffic

fila
traffic jam

parkeerplaats
car park

stacion di trein
train station

riel
tracks

trein
train

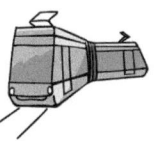

tram
tram

wagon
carriage

helicopter

helicopter

aeropuerto

airport

toren

tower

pasahero

passenger

container

container

caha di carton

carton

garoshi

cart

macutu

basket

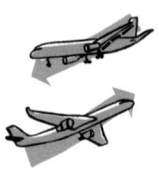

lanta / baha

take off / land

ciudad

city

pueblo

village

centro di ciudad

city centre

cas

house

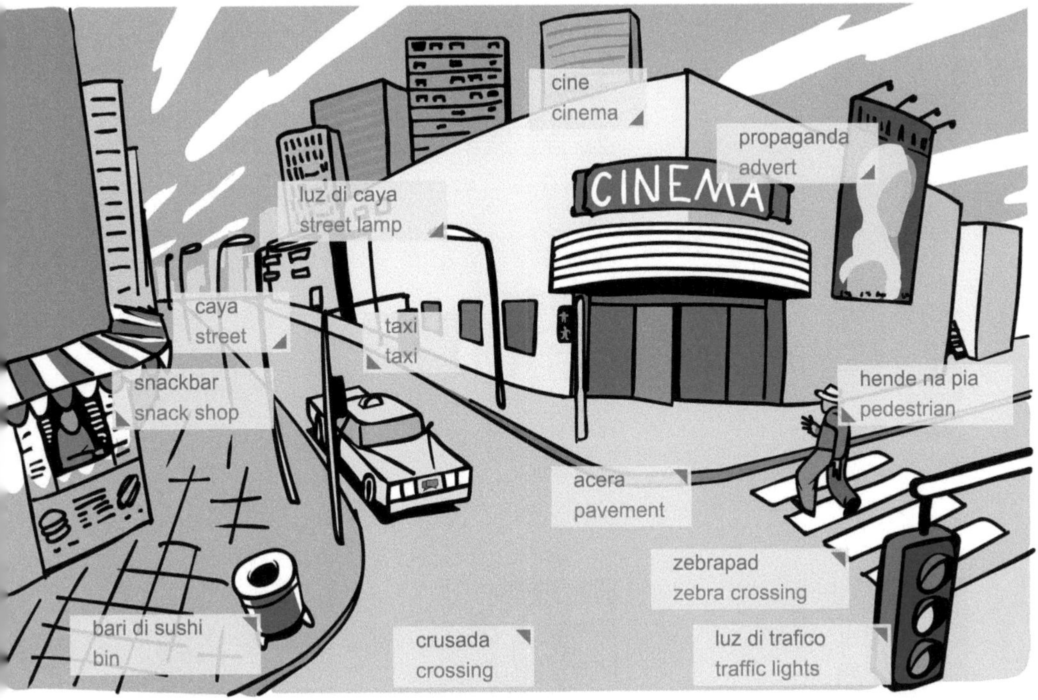

cine
cinema
CINEMA
propaganda
advert
luz di caya
street lamp
caya
street
taxi
taxi
snackbar
snack shop
hende na pia
pedestrian
acera
pavement
zebrapad
zebra crossing
bari di sushi
bin
crusada
crossing
luz di trafico
traffic lights

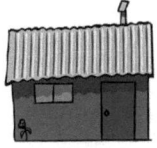

hut

hut

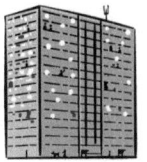

flat

flat

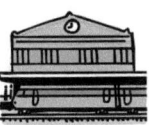

stacion di trein

train station

stadhuis

town hall

MUSEUM

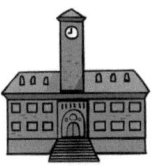

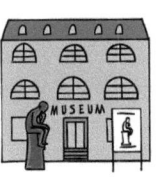

museo

museum

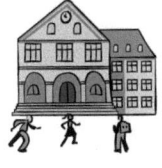

scol

school

universidad

university

banco

bank

hospital

hospital

hotel

hotel

botica

pharmacy

oficina

office

boekhandel

book shop

tienda

shop

floresteria

florist's

supermarket

supermarket

mercado

market

department store

department store

bendedo di pisca

fishmonger's

shopping center

shopping centre

haf

harbour

park
park

banki
bench

brug
bridge

trapi
stairs

metro
underground

tunnel
tunnel

parada di bus
bus stop

bar
bar

restaurant
restaurant

postbox
postbox

borchi di nomber di caya
street sign

parkeermeter
parking meter

parke di bestia
zoo

piscina
swimming pool

moskee
mosque

cunucu

farm

polucion

pollution

santana

graveyard

misa

church

speelplaats

playground

tempel

temple

paisahe
landscape

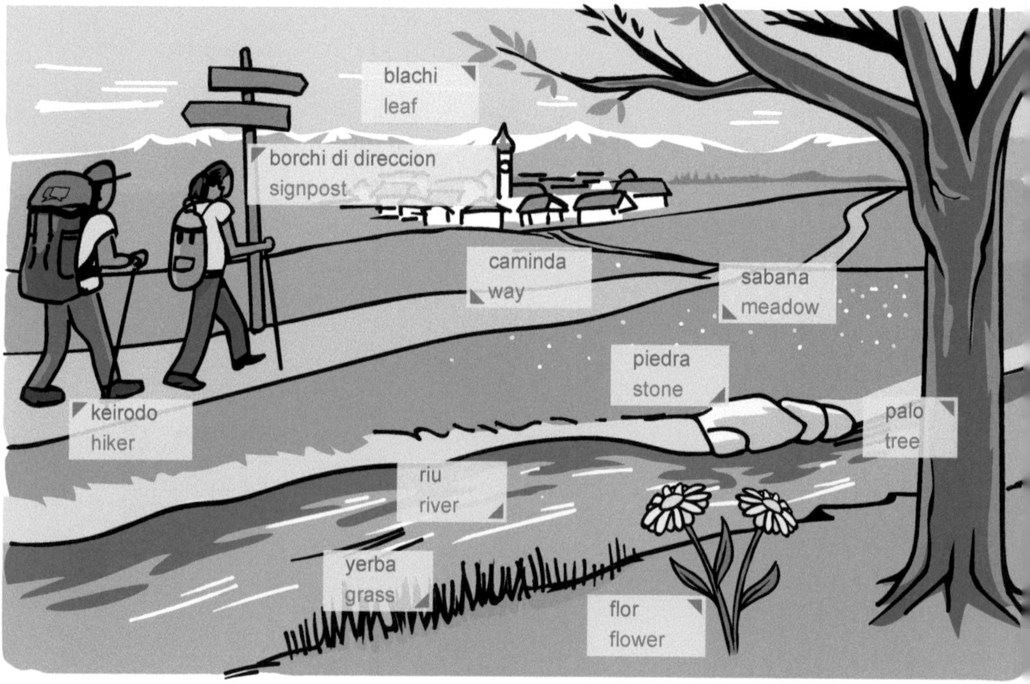

blachi
leaf

borchi di direccion
signpost

caminda
way

sabana
meadow

piedra
stone

keirodo
hiker

palo
tree

riu
river

yerba
grass

flor
flower

vallei

valley

sero

hill

lago

lake

mondi

forest

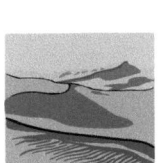

desierto

desert

volcan

volcano

kasteel

castle

arco iris

rainbow

paddenstoel

mushroom

palma

palm tree

sangura

mosquito

musca

fly

vruminga

ant

bij

bee

haraña

spider

tor

beetle

dori

frog

eekhoorn

squirrel

porcospina

hedgehog

coneu

hare

shoco

owl

parha

bird

zwaan

swan

porco di mondi

boar

bina

deer

eland

moose

dam

dam

molina di biento

wind turbine

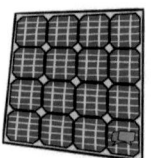

panel solar

solar panel

clima

climate

restaurant
restaurant

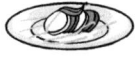

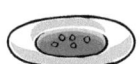

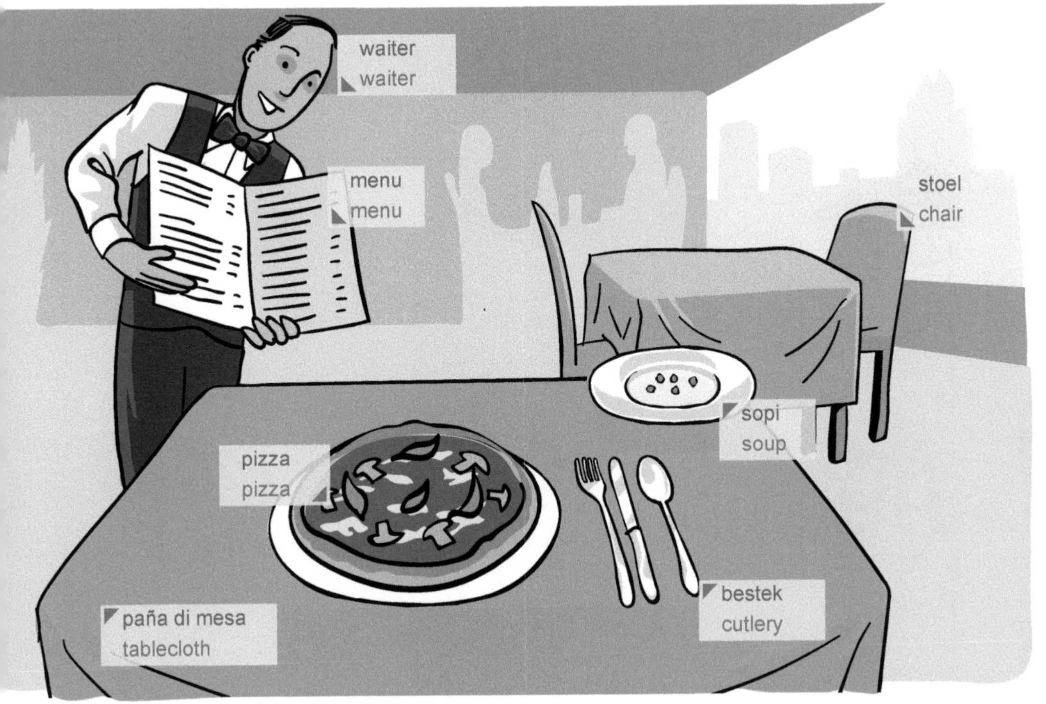
waiter
waiter
menu
menu
stoel
chair
sopi
soup
pizza
pizza
bestek
cutlery
paña di mesa
tablecloth

aperitivo

starter

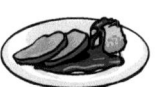

cuminda principal

main course

dessert

dessert

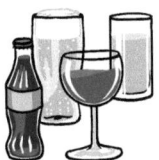

bebida

drinks

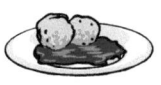

cuminda

food

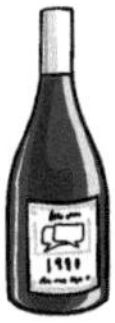

boter

bottle

fastfood

fast food

streetfood

street food

canica di te

teapot

pochi di sucu

sugar bowl

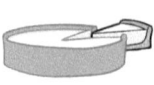

porcion

portion

espressomachine

espresso machine

stoel di mucha

high chair

cuenta

bill

hasechi

tray

cuchiu

knife

forki

fork

cuchara

spoon

telep

teaspoon

napkin

serviette

glas

glass

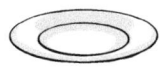

tayo
plate

tayo di sopi
soup plate

scoter
saucer

saus
sauce

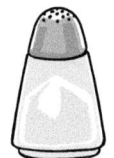

pochi di salo
salt pot

mulina di peper
pepper mill

binager
vinegar

azeta
oil

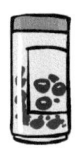

specerij
spices

ketchup
ketchup

mosterd
mustard

mayonaise
mayonnaise

supermarket
supermarket

oferta special
special offer
cliente
customer
producto lacteo
dairy
FOR
fruta
fruit
garoshi di compra
trolley

BUTCHERS

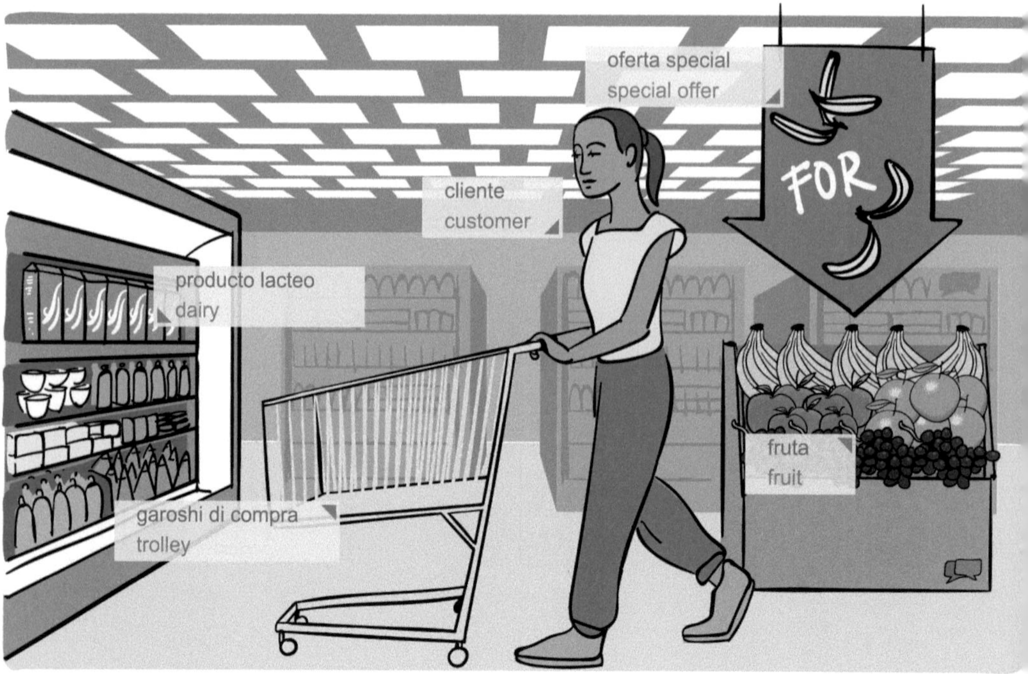

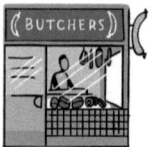

carniceria

butcher´s

BAKERY

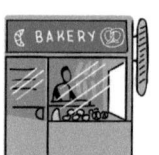

panaderia

baker´s

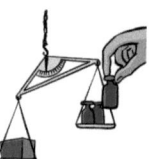

pisa

weigh

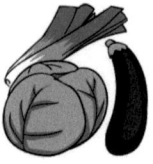

berdura

vegetables

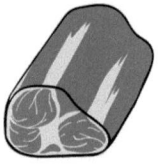

carni

meat

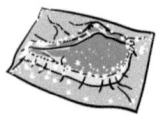

frozen food

frozen food

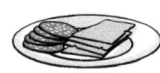

beleg di carni

cold meat

cuminda di bleki

tinned food

detergente na puiro

washing powder

mangel

sweets

producto pa cas

household products

articulo di limpiesa

cleaning products

bendedo

salesperson

cahero

till

cahero

cashier

lista di compra

shopping list

orario

opening hours

cartera

wallet

credit card

credit card

tas

bag

saco di plastic

plastic bag

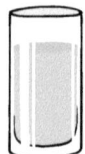

awa

water

juice

juice

lechi

milk

cola

coke

biña

wine

cerbes

beer

alcohol

alcohol

chocomel

cocoa

te

tea

koffie

coffee

espresso

espresso

cappuccino

cappuccino

bacoba

banana

appel

apple

apelsina

orange

milon

melon

lamunchi

lemon

wortel

carrot

conoflok

garlic

bambu

bamboo

siboyo

onion

mushroom

mushroom

noot

nuts

pasta

noodles

spaghetti

spaghetti

aros

rice

salada

salad

batata hasa

chips

batata hasa

fried potatoes

pizza

pizza

hamburger

hamburger

sandwich

sandwich

cutlet

cutlet

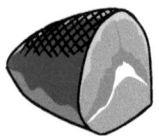

ham

ham

salami

salami

soseishi

sausage

galiña

chicken

hasa

roast

pisca

fish

papa

porridge oats

müsli

muesli

cornflakes

cornflakes

hariña

flour

croissant

croissant

pan rondo

bread roll

pan

bread

toast

toast

cuki

biscuits

manteca

butter

kwark

curd

bolo

cake

webo

egg

webo hasa

fried egg

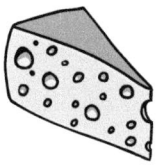

keshi

cheese

ijscream

ice cream

sucu

sugar

honing

honey

jam

jam

pasta di chuculati

chocolate spread

curry

curry

cunucu

farm

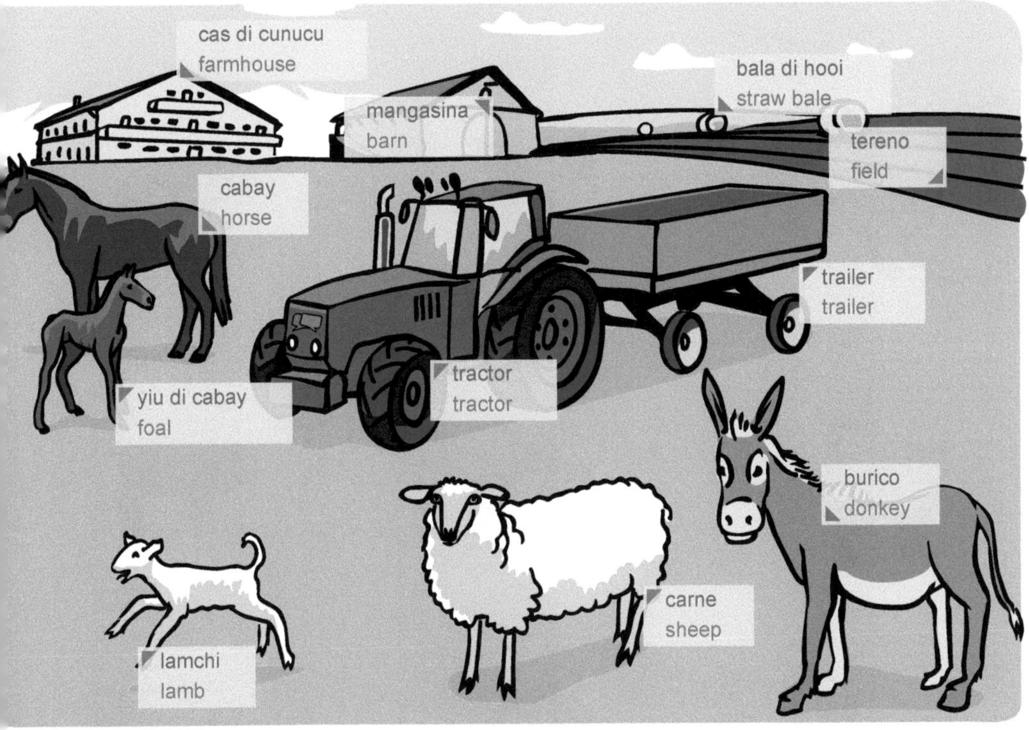
cas di cunucu
farmhouse
mangasina
barn
bala di hooi
straw bale
tereno
field
cabay
horse
trailer
trailer
tractor
tractor
yiu di cabay
foal
burico
donkey
carne
sheep
lamchi
lamb

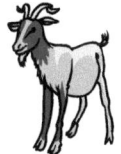

cabrito

goat

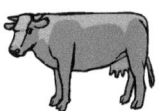

baca

cow

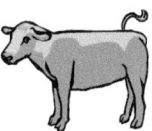

bishe

calf

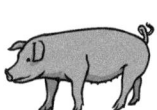

porco

pig

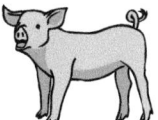

yiu di porco

piglet

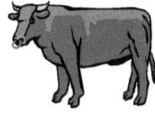

toro

bull

gans
goose

pato
duck

puyito
chick

galiña
hen

gay
cock

djaca
rat

pushi
cat

raton
mouse

toro
ox

cacho
dog

cas di cacho
doghouse

slang pa muha mata
garden hose

gieter
watering can

herment pa corta yerbe
scythe

ploeg
plough

garabati
....
sickle

chapi
....
hoe

forki pa coy hooi
....
pitchfork

hacha
....
axe

garetia
....
wheelbarrow

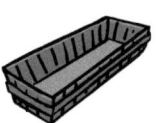

pesebre
....
trough

canica di lechi
....
milk can

saco
....
sack

heki
....
fence

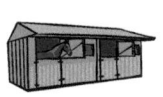

stal
....
stable

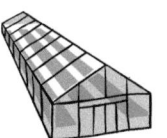

greenhouse
....
greenhouse

suela
....
soil

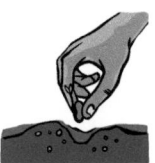

simia
....
seed

mest
....
fertilizer

mashin di cosecha
....
combine harvester

cosecha

harvest

cosecha

harvest

yams

yams

trigo

wheat

soya

soy

batata

potato

maishi

corn

canola

rapeseed

palo di fruta

fruit tree

yuca

cassava

grano

cereals

cas
house

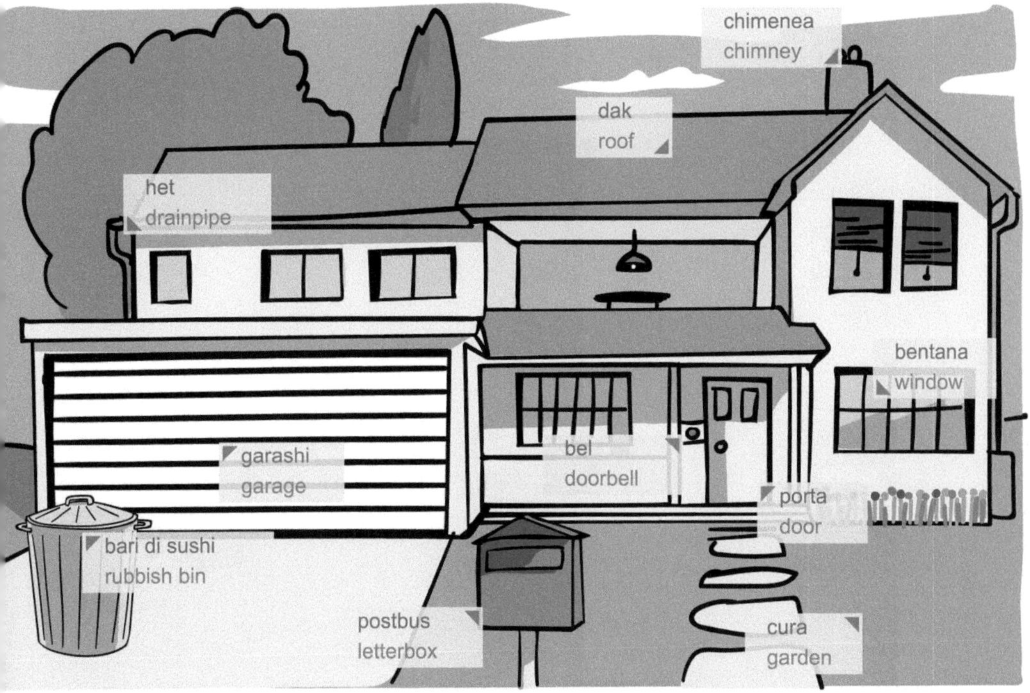

chimenea
chimney
dak
roof
het
drainpipe
bentana
window
garashi
garage
bel
doorbell
porta
door
bari di sushi
rubbish bin
postbus
letterbox
cura
garden

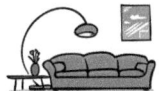

sala

living room

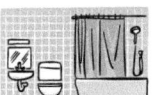

baño

bathroom

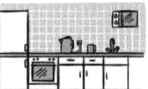

cushina

kitchen

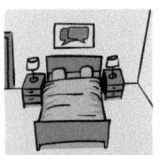

camber

bedroom

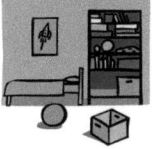

camber di mucha

child's room

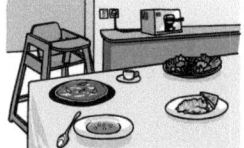

comedo

dining room

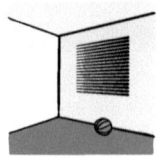

suela

floor

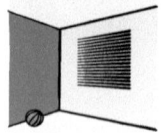

muraya

wall

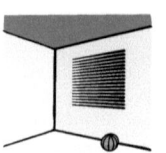

blafon

ceiling

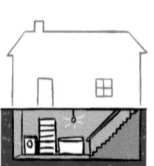

bodega

cellar

sauna

sauna

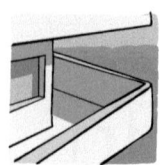

balcon

balcony

terasa

terrace

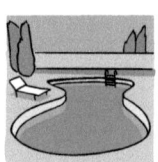

piscina

pool

mashin di corta yerba

lawn mower

laken

sheet

bedsprei

bedspread

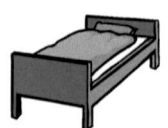

cama

bed

basora

broom

hemchi

bucket

switch

switch

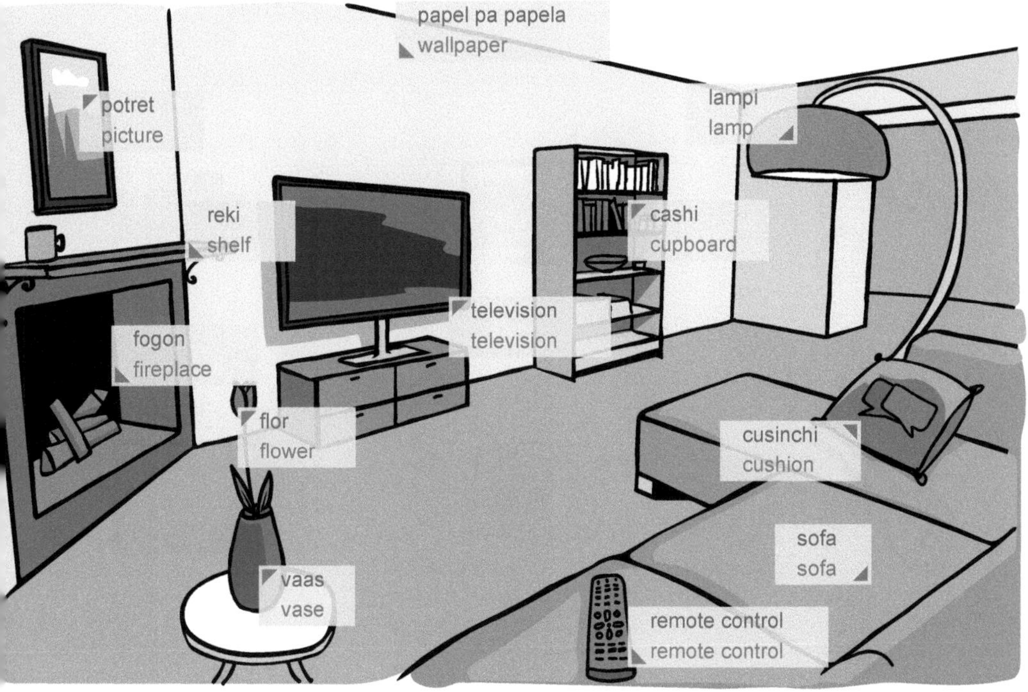

papel pa papela
wallpaper

potret
picture

lampi
lamp

reki
shelf

cashi
cupboard

fogon
fireplace

television
television

flor
flower

cusinchi
cushion

vaas
vase

sofa
sofa

remote control
remote control

tapijt

carpet

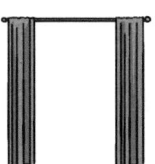

cortina

curtain

mesa

table

stoel

chair

stoel di zoya

rocking chair

stoel

armchair

buki

book

dekel

blanket

decoracion

decoration

palo pa kima

firewood

film

film

stereoset

hi-fi equipment

yabi

key

corant

newspaper

cuadra

painting

poster

poster

radio

radio

blocnote

notepad

stofzuiger

hoover

cadushi

cactus

bela

candle

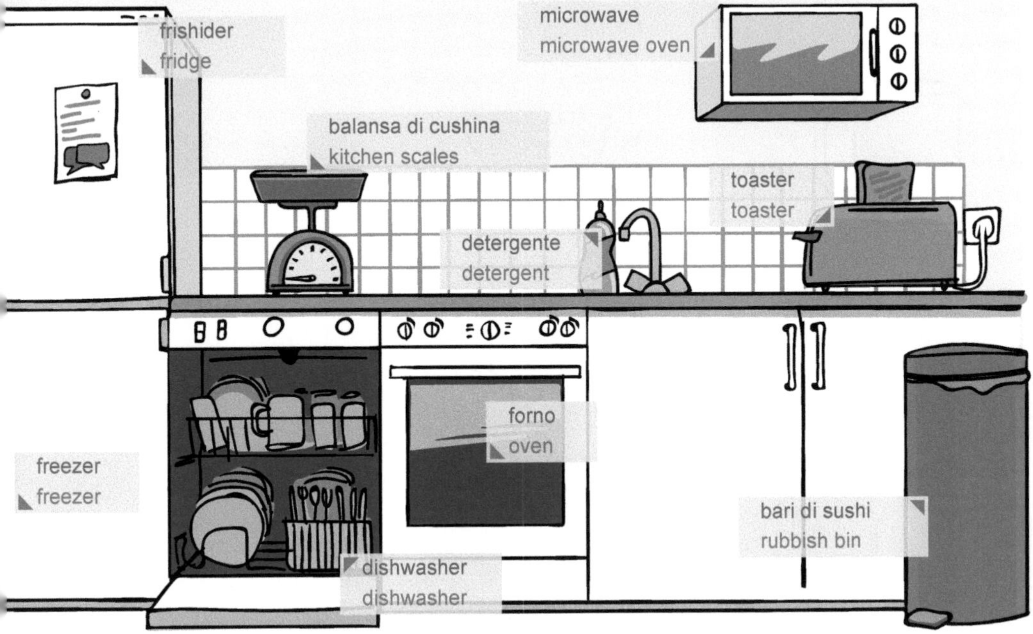

frishider
fridge

microwave
microwave oven

balansa di cushina
kitchen scales

toaster
toaster

detergente
detergent

freezer
freezer

forno
oven

bari di sushi
rubbish bin

dishwasher
dishwasher

stoof	wea	wea di hero
cooker	pot	cast-iron pot

wok	planchi	ketel
wok / kadai	pan	kettle

steamer

steamer

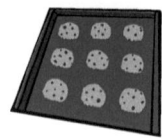

teblachi pa horna

baking tray

servies

crockery

beker

mug

conchi

bowl

chopstick

chopsticks

cuchara di sopi

ladle

spatula

spatula

garde

whisk

scurido

strainer

colado

sieve

raspa

grater

fenso

mortar

barbecue

barbecue

candela

open fire

planki pa corta

chopping board

rostok

rolling pin

kurkentrek

corkscrew

bleki

can

cos di habri bleki

can opener

pannenlap

pot holder

wasbak

sink

skeiro

brush

spons

sponge

blender

blender

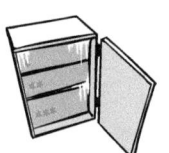

freezer

deep freezer

tetero

baby bottle

cranchi

tap

baño

bathroom

verwarming
heating

douche
shower

serbete
towel

cortina di douche
shower curtain

baño di scuma
bubble bath

badkuip
bathtub

glas
glass

wasmashin
washing machine

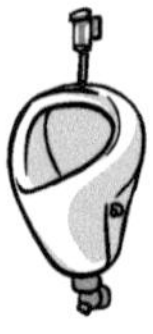

cranchi
tap

mosaik
tiles

pot
potty

wasbak
sink

tualet	hurktoilet	bidet
toilet	squat toilet	bidet
urinal	papel di w.c.	skeiro di w.c.
urinal	toilet paper	toilet brush

skeiro di djente

toothbrush

pasta di djente

toothpaste

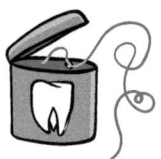

dental floss

dental floss

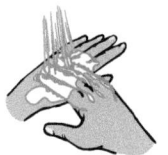

laba

wash

douche di man

handheld shower

bidet

douche

tobo

basin

skeiro

back brush

habon

soap

shower gel

shower gel

shampoo

shampoo

washandje

flannel

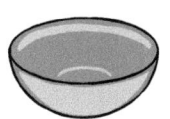

drain

drain

crema

cream

desodorante

deodorant

spiel

mirror

spiel di man

hand mirror

blet

razor

shaving foam

shaving foam

aftershave

aftershave

peña

comb

skeiro

brush

blower

hair dryer

spray pa cabey

hairspray

makeup

makeup

lipstick

lipstick

cos di pinta huña

nail varnish

catuna

cotton wool

sker pa corta huña

nail scissors

perfume

perfume

tas

washbag

kruk

stool

balansa

weighing scale

bata

bathrobe

handschoen

rubber gloves

tampon

tampon

kotex

sanitary towel

wc kimico

chemical toilet

camber di mucha
child's room

wekker
alarm clock
peluche
cuddly toy
auto di hunga
toy car
maraca
rattle
cas di popchi
doll's house
regalo
present

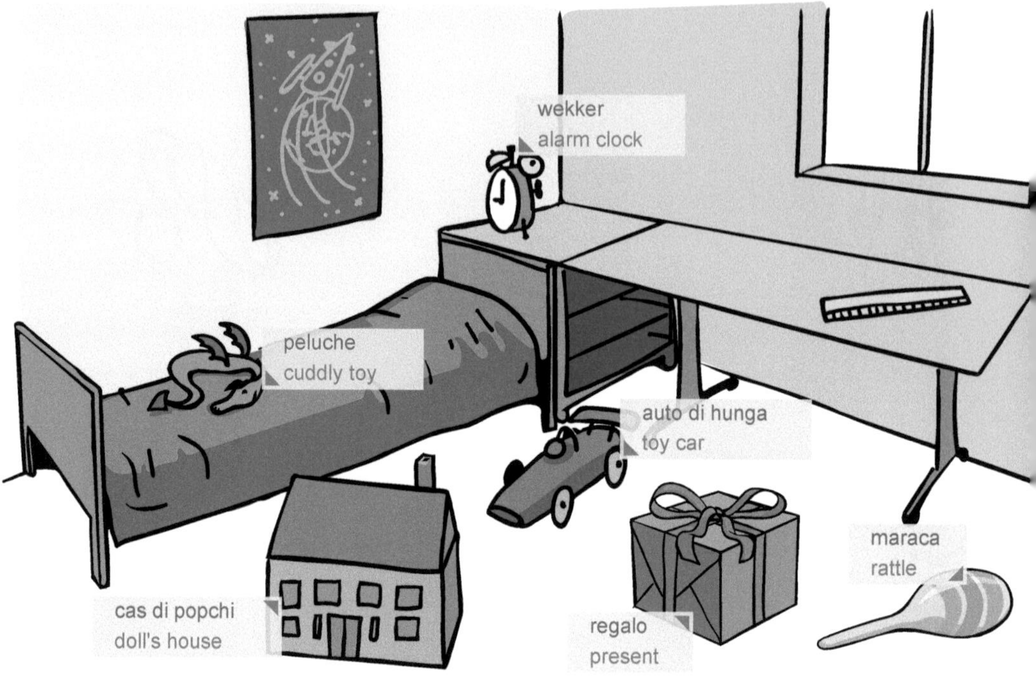

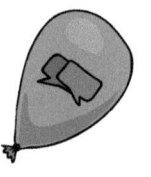

blaas

balloon

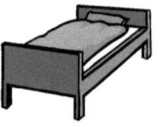

cama

bed

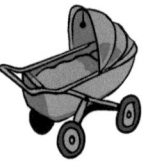

stroller

pram

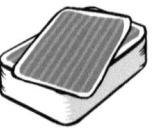

baraha di carta

deck of cards

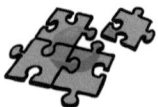

puzzel

jigsaw

comic

comic

lego
lego bricks

bloki di hunga
building blocks

figura di accion
action figure

romper
babygrow

frisbee
frisbee

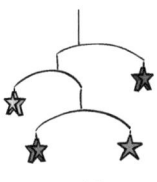

mobil
mobile

wega di mesa
board game

dou
dice

set di trein
model train set

chupon
dummy

fiesta
party

buki di prenchi
picture book

bala
ball

popchi
doll

hunga
play

zandbak

sandpit

zoya

swing

cos di hunga

toys

videogame

video game console

tricycle

tricycle

beer

teddy bear

cashi di paña

wardrobe

paña
clothing

mea

socks

mea

stockings

pantyhose

tights

sjaal
scarf

paraplu
umbrella

faha
belt

T-shirt
t-shirt

boots
boots

slof
slippers

keds
trainers

sandalia
·················
sandals

sapato
·················
shoes

laars di rubber
·················
rubber boots

carsonsio
·················
underpants

bh
·················
bra

flanel
·················
vest

body
body

carson
trousers

jeans
jeans

saya
skirt

blusa
blouse

camisa
shirt

sweater
pullover

sweater
hoodie

blazer
blazer

jacket
jacket

jas
coat

regenjas
raincoat

flus
costume

shimis
dress

shimis di bruid
wedding dress

flus

suit

yapon

nightgown

pidjama

pyjamas

sari

sari

lenso di cabes

headscarf

turban

turban

burqa

burqa

kaftan

kaftan

abaya

abaya

zwempak

swimsuit

zwembroek

trunks

carson cortico

shorts

trainingspak

tracksuit

lantera

apron

handschoen

gloves

boton

button

bril

glasses

armband

bracelet

cadena

necklace

renchi

ring

renchi di horea

earring

pechi

cap

kapstok

coat hanger

sombre

hat

dashi

tie

ziper

zip

helm

helmet

guiel

braces

uniform di scol

school uniform

uniform

uniform

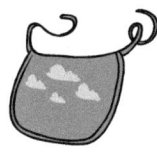

babado

bib

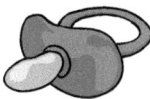

chupon

dummy

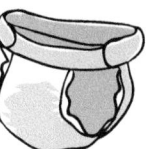

bruki

nappy

oficina
office

server
server
filekast
filing cabinet
printer
printer
papel
paper
pantaya
monitor
lessenaar
desk
mouse
mouse
map
folder
keyboard
keyboard
stoel
chair
bari di sushi
waste-paper basket
computer
computer

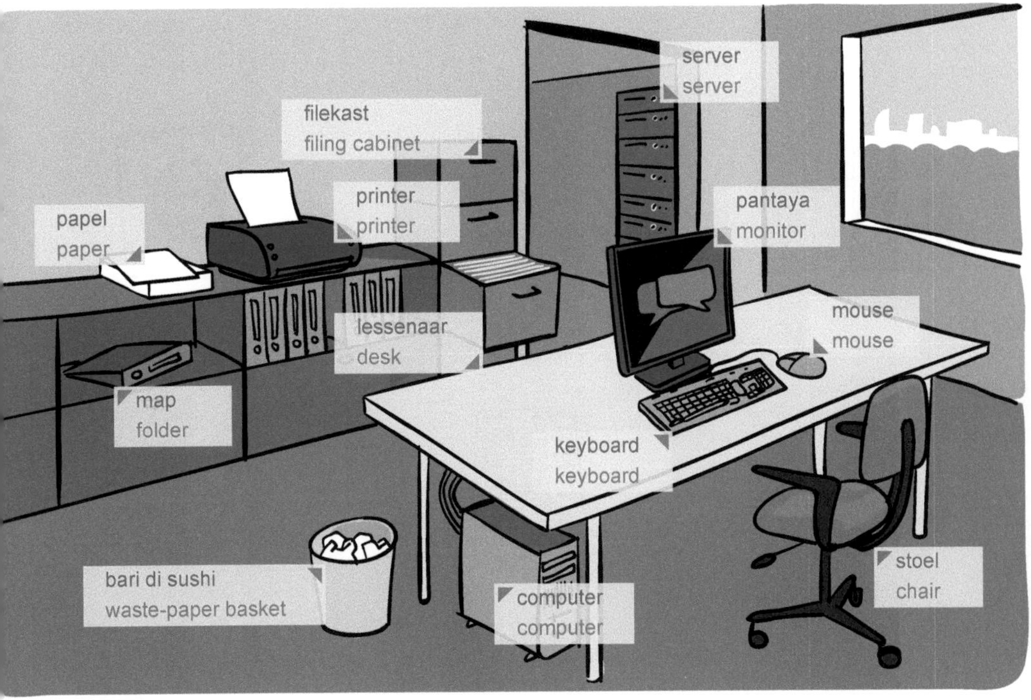

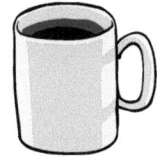

copi pa bebe koffie

coffee mug

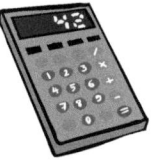

calculator

calculator

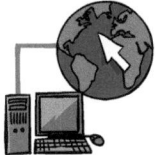

internet

internet

laptop
laptop

carta
letter

mensahe
message

celular
mobile

red
network

mashin di copia
photocopier

software
software

telefon
telephone

stopcontact
plug socket

fax mashin
fax machine

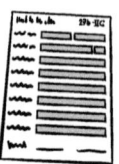

formulario
form

documento
document

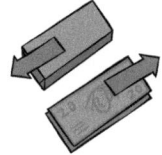

cumpra
buy

paga
pay

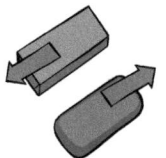

negosha
trade

placa
money

dollar
dollar

euro
euro

yen
yen

roebel
rouble

frank suiso
Swiss franc

yuan renminbi
renminbi yuan

roepi
rupee

bancomatico
cashpoint

oficina di cambio

bureau de change

oro

gold

plata

silver

azeta

oil

energia

energy

prijs

price

contract

contract

impuesto

tax

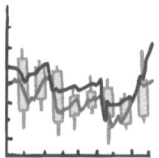

share

stock

traha

work

empleado

employee

dunado di trabou

employer

fabrica

factory

tienda

shop

ofishi / profesion
occupations

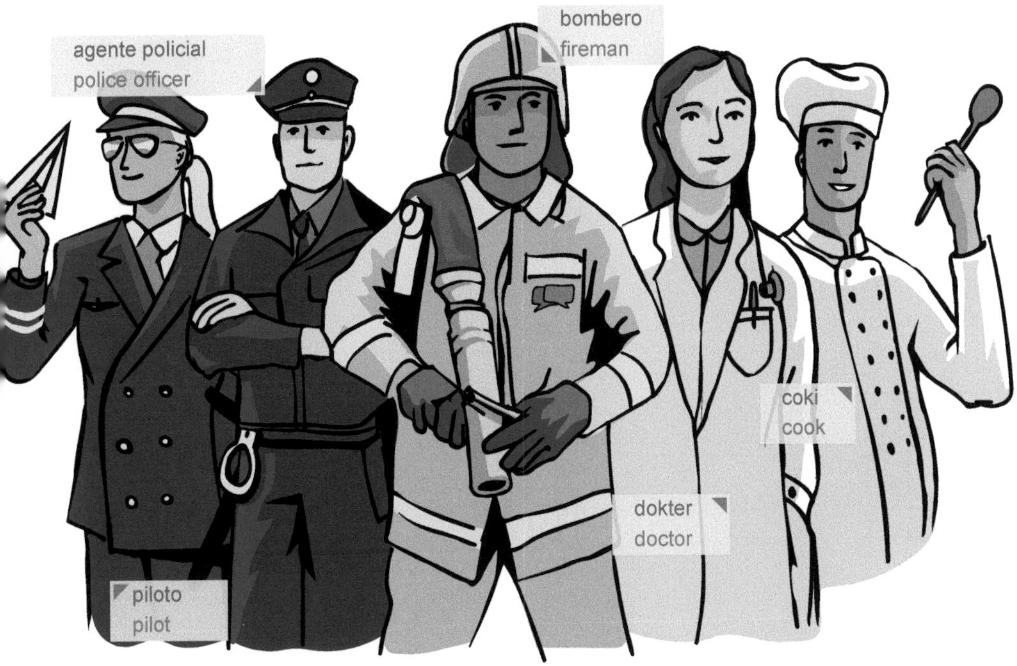

agente policial
police officer
bombero
fireman
coki
cook
dokter
doctor
piloto
pilot

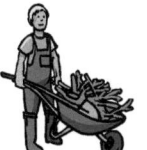

hardinero

gardener

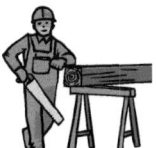

carpinte

carpenter

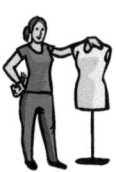

cosedo

seamstress

hues

judge

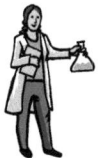

kimico

chemist

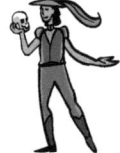

actor

actor

chauffeur di bus

bus driver

chauffeur di taxi

taxi driver

piscado

fisherman

hende cu ta haci cas limpi

cleaning lady

drechado di dak

roofer

waiter

waiter

jaagdo

hunter

verfdo

painter

panadero

baker

electricista

electrician

trahado den construccion

builder

ingeniero

engineer

carnicero

butcher

loodgieter

plumber

partido di carta

postman

solda
soldier

arkitecto
architect

cahero
cashier

florista
florist

pelukero / pelukera
hairdresser

controlado di ticket
conductor

mecanico
mechanic

capitan
captain

dentista
dentist

cientifico
scientist

rabbi
rabbi

imam
imam

monk
monk

pastor
clergyman

herment

tools

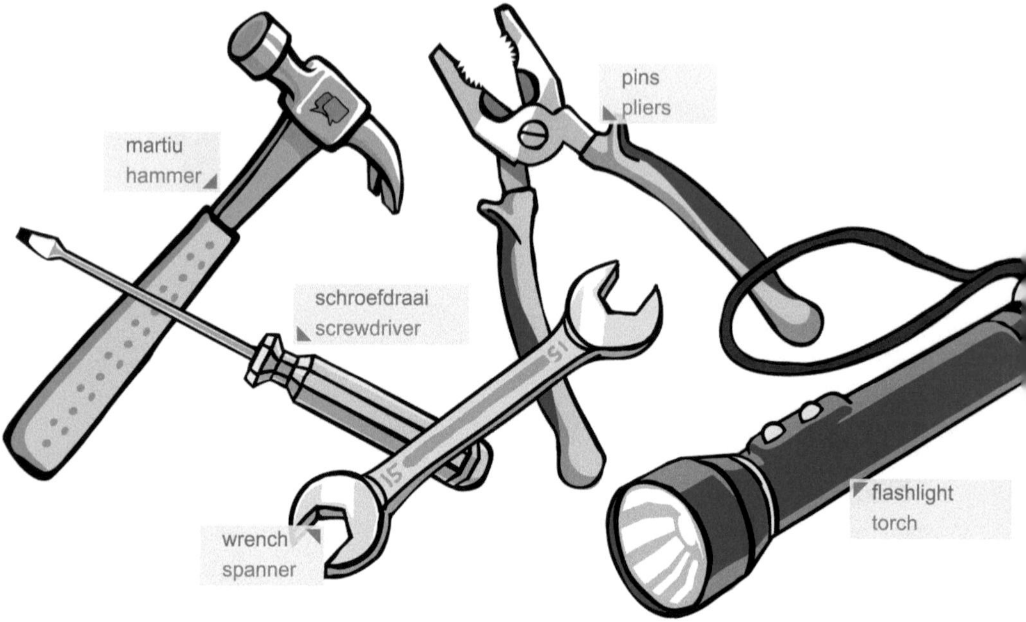

martiu
hammer
pins
pliers
schroefdraai
screwdriver
wrench
spanner
flashlight
torch

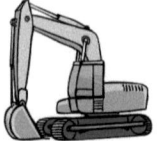

bulldozer

digger

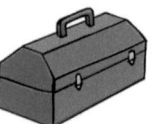

caha di herment

toolbox

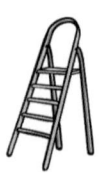

trapi

ladder

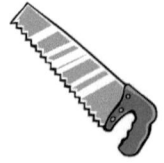

zaag

saw

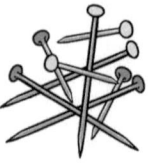

clabo

nails

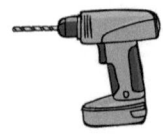

boormashin

drill

drecha
repair

shobel
shovel

caraho!
Damn!

scop
dustpan

bleki di verf
paint pot

schroef
screws

instrumento musical
musical instruments

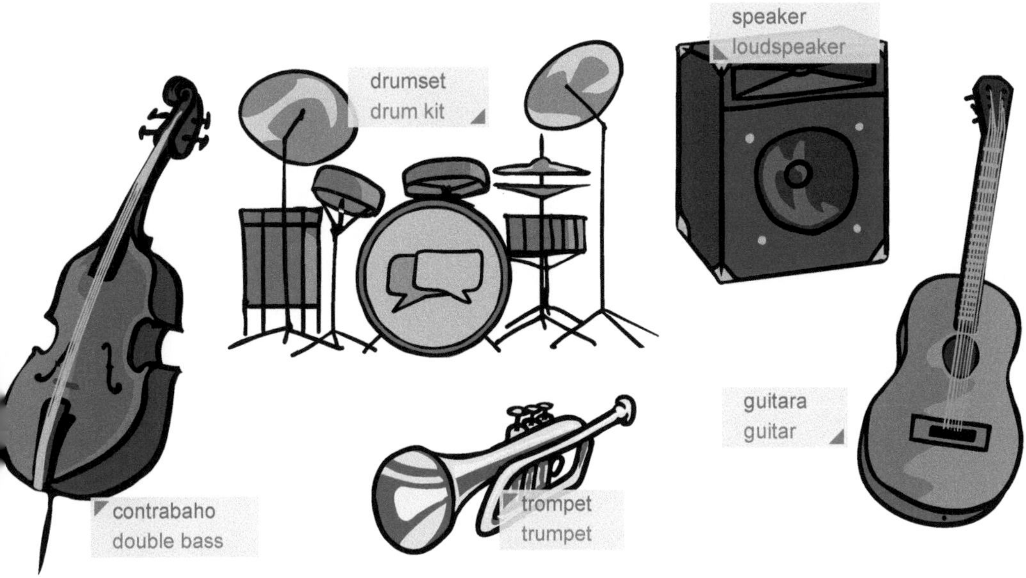

drumset
drum kit

speaker
loudspeaker

guitara
guitar

contrabaho
double bass

trompet
trumpet

piano

piano

fio

violin

baho

bass

timbal

timpani

tambu

drums

keyboard

keyboard

saxofon

saxophone

fluit

flute

microfon

microphone

parke di bestia

zoo

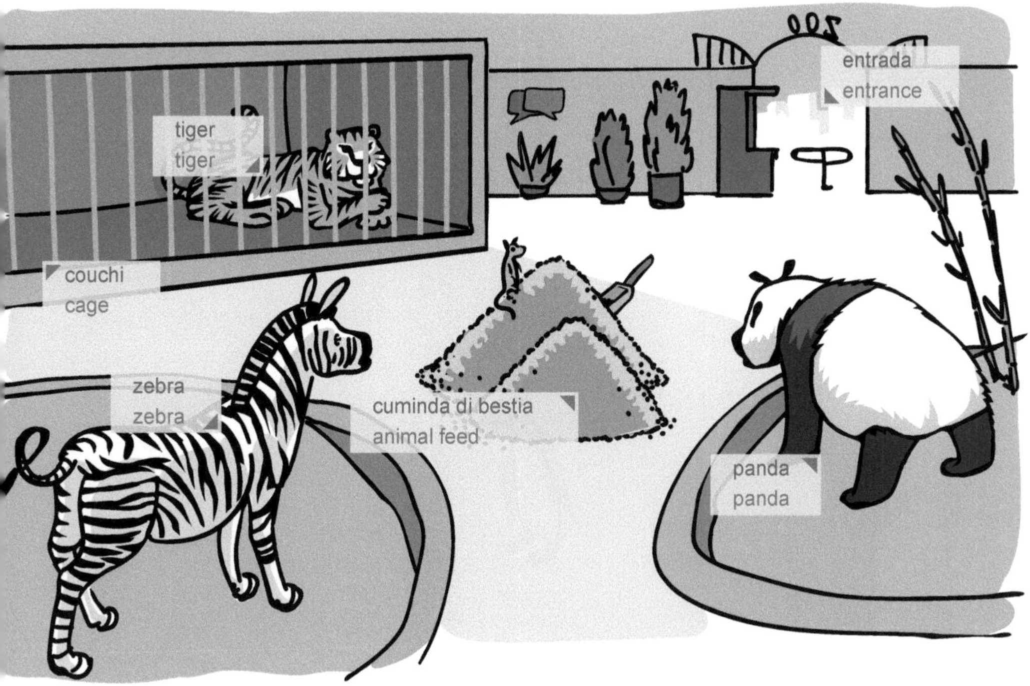

tiger
tiger
couchi
cage
zebra
zebra
cuminda di bestia
animal feed
panda
panda
entrada
entrance

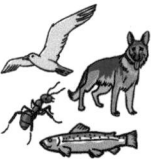

animal

animals

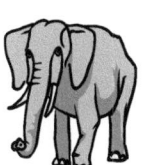

olifante

elephant

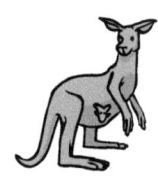

cangaru

kangaroo

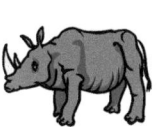

neushoorn

rhino

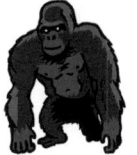

gorila

gorilla

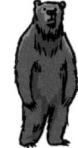

beer

bear

camel

camel

avestruz

ostrich

leon

lion

macaco

monkey

flamingo

flamingo

lora

parrot

beer polar

polar bear

pinguin

penguin

tribon

shark

pauwies

peacock

colebra

snake

caiman

crocodile

cuidado di bestia

zookeeper

cacho di awa

seal

jaguar

jaguar

pony
pony

leopardo
leopard

hipopotamo
hippo

giraf
giraffe

aguila
eagle

porco di mondi
boar

pisca
fish

turtuga
turtle

walrus
walrus

vos
fox

gazelle
gazelle

futbol Americano
American football

ciclismo
cycling

tennis
tennis

basketball
basketball

landamento
swimming

boxeo
boxing

ice hockey
ice hockey

futbol
football

badminton
badminton

atletismo
athletics

handbal
handball

ski
skiing

polo
polo

actividad
activities

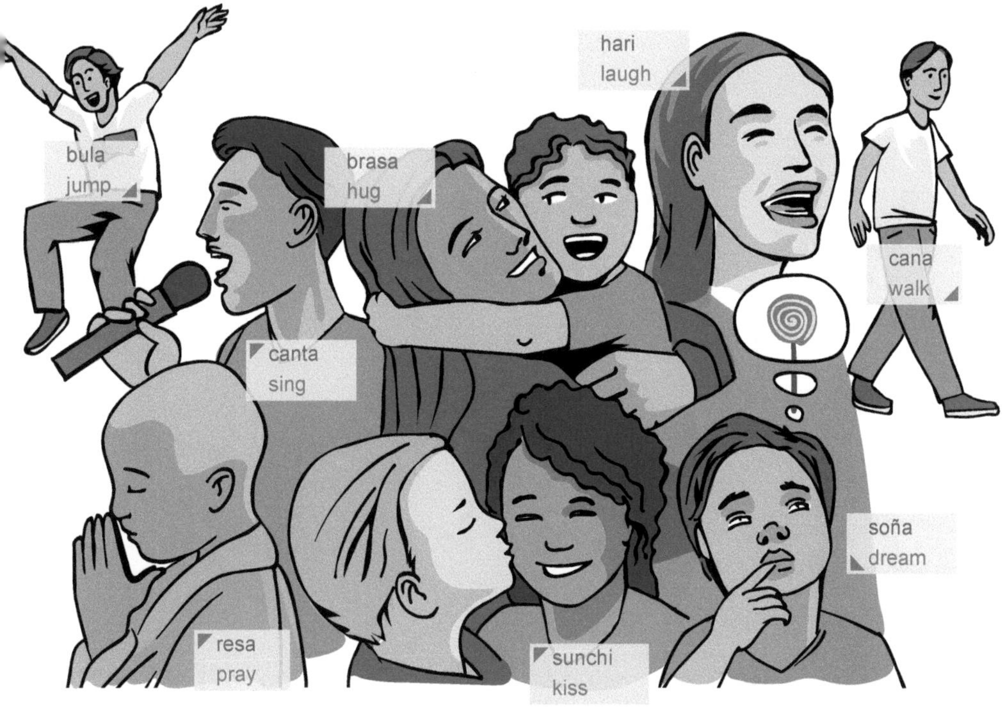
hari
laugh
bula
jump
brasa
hug
cana
walk
canta
sing
soña
dream
resa
pray
sunchi
kiss

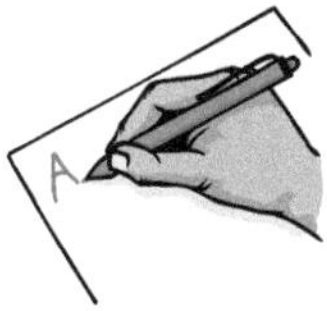

skirbi

write

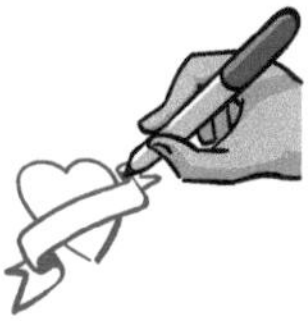

pinta

draw

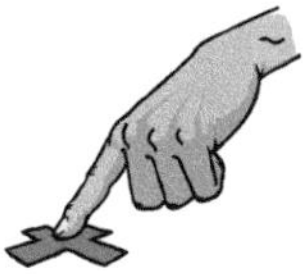

mustra

show

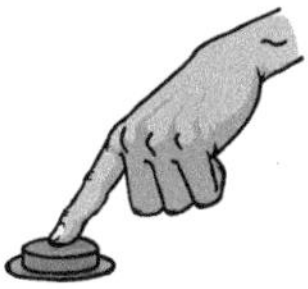

primi

push

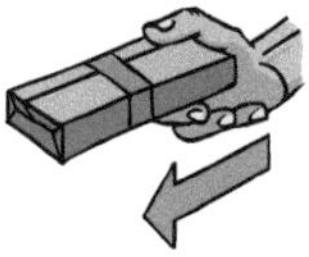

duna

give

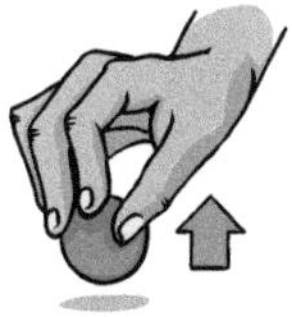

coy

take

tin

have

haci

do

ta

be

para

stand

core

run

ranca

pull

tira

throw

cay

fall

drumi

lie

warda

wait

carga

carry

sinta

sit

bisti

get dressed

drumi

sleep

lanta fo'i soño

wake up

mira

look at

yora

cry

caricia

stroke

peña

comb

papia

talk

compronde

understand

puntra

ask

scucha

listen

bebe

drink

come

eat

ruim op

tidy up

stima

love

cushna

cook

bai

drive

bula

fly

actividad - activities

zeilo

sail

conta

calculate

lesa

read

siña

learn

traha

work

casa

marry

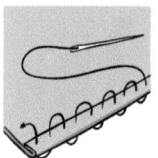

cose

sew

skeiro djente

brush teeth

mata

kill

huma

smoke

manda

send

famia

family

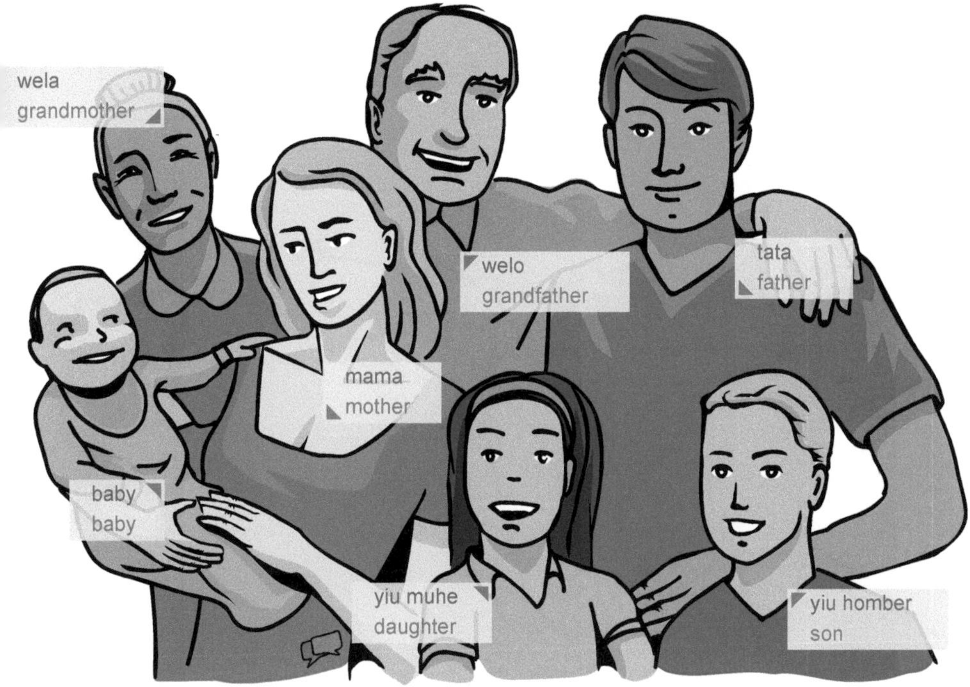

wela
grandmother
welo
grandfather
tata
father
mama
mother
baby
baby
yiu muhe
daughter
yiu homber
son

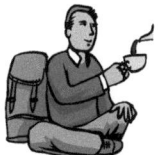

huesped

guest

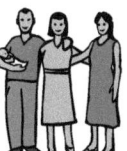

tanta

aunt

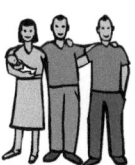

omo

uncle

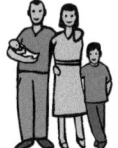

ruman homber

brother

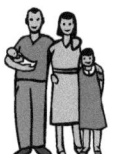

ruman muhe

sister

curpa

body

frenta
forehead
wowo
eye
schouder
shoulder
dede
finger
cara
face
cachete
chin
man
hand
pecho
breast
pia
leg
brasa
arm

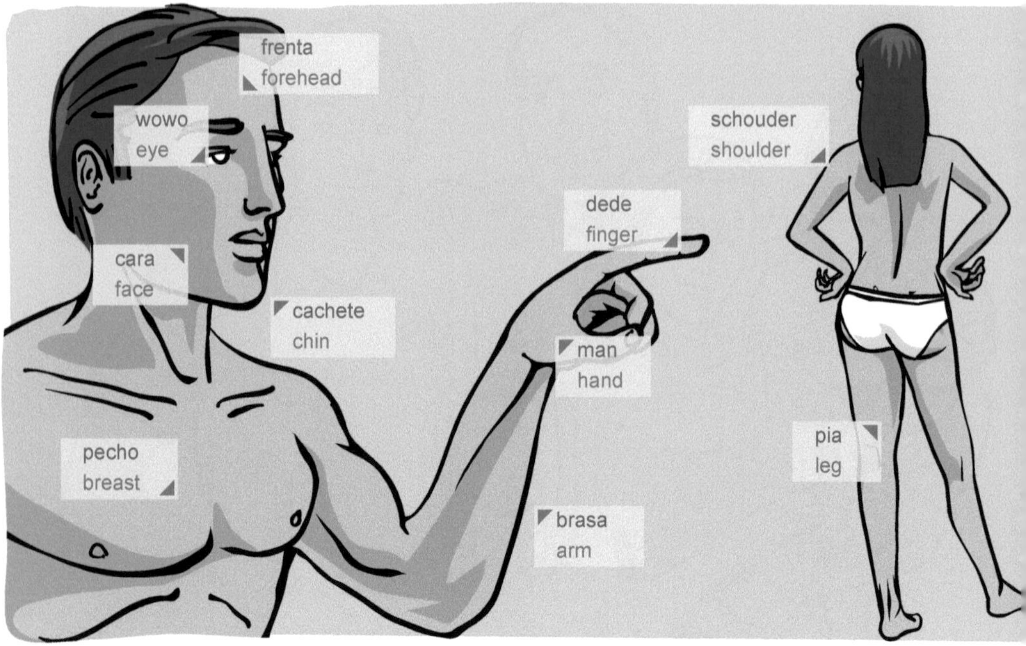

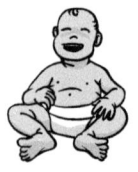

baby

baby

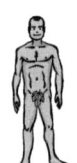

homber

man

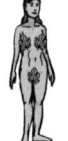

muhe

woman

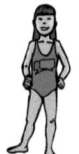

mucha muhe

girl

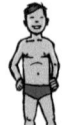

mucha homber

boy

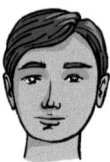

cabes

head

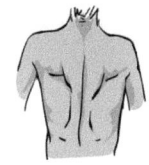

lomba

back

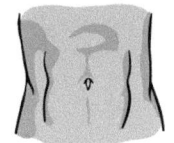

bariga

belly

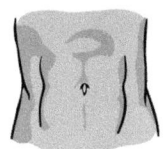

lombrishi

belly button

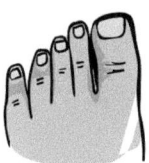

dede di pia

toe

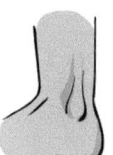

hilchi

heel

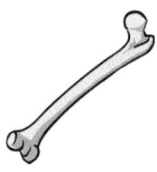

weso

bone

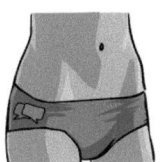

heup

hip

rudia

knee

elleboog

elbow

nanishi

nose

chanchan

bottom

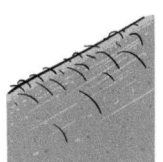

cuero

skin

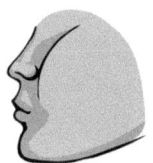

wang

cheek

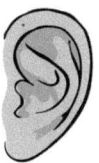

horea

ear

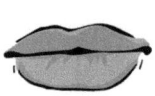

lip

lip

boca

mouth

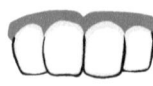

djente

tooth

lenga

tongue

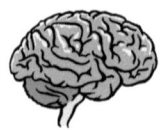

celebro

brain

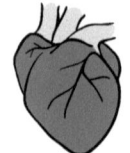

curason

heart

musculo

muscle

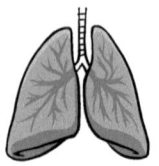

pulmon

lung

higra

liver

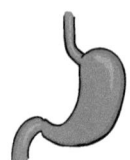

stoma

stomach

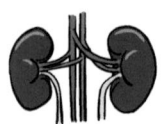

nier

kidneys

sex

sex

condon

condom

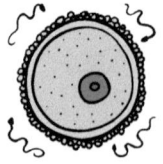

ovulo

ovum

sperma

semen

embaraso

pregnancy

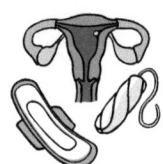

menstruacion
....
menstruation

vagina
....
vagina

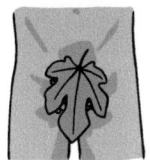

penis
....
penis

wenkbrauw
....
eyebrow

cabey
....
hair

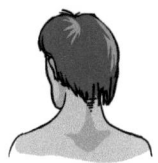

nek
....
neck

hospital

hospital

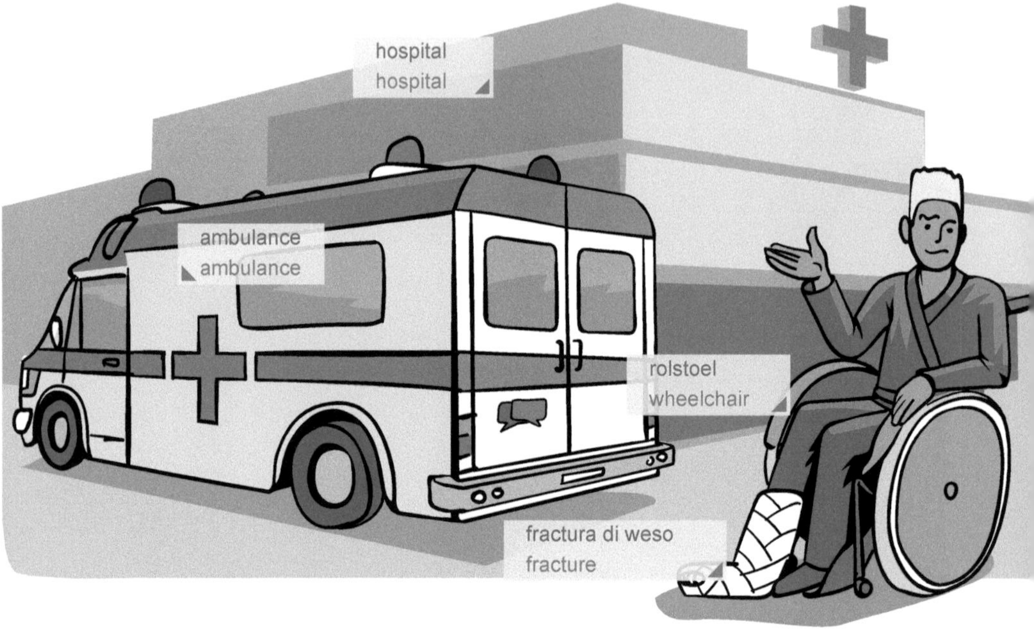

hospital
hospital
ambulance
ambulance
rolstoel
wheelchair
fractura di weso
fracture

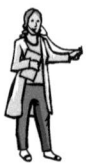

dokter
doctor

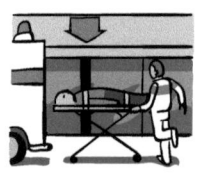

EHBO (prome asistencia/eerste hulp)
emergency room

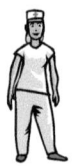

nurse
nurse

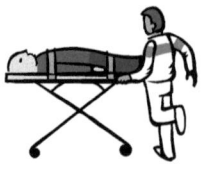

caso di emergencia
emergency

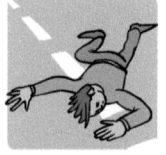

fo'i tino
unconscious

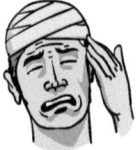

dolor
pain

lesion

injury

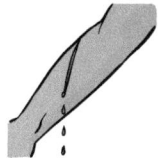

sangramento

bleeding

ataca di curason

heart attack

ataca celebral

stroke

alergia

allergy

tosa

cough

keintura

fever

griep

flu

diarea

diarrhoea

dolor di cabes

headache

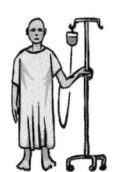

cancer

cancer

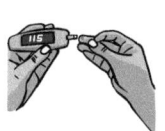

diabetes

diabetes

ciruhano

surgeon

scalpel

scalpel

operacion

operation

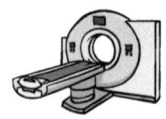

CT

CT

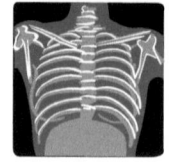

x-ray

x-ray

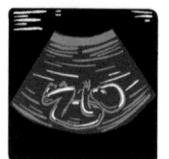

echo

ultrasound

masker contra stof

face mask

malesa

disease

sala di espera

waiting room

kruk

crutch

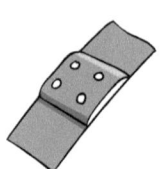

pleister

plaster

verband

bandage

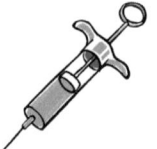

inyeccion

injection

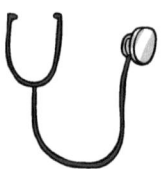

stetoscop

stethoscope

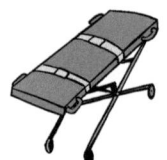

brancard

stretcher

thermometer

clinical thermometer

nacemento

birth

sobrepeso

overweight

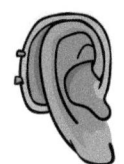

aparato pa oido

hearing aid

desinfectante

disinfectant

infeccion

infection

virus

virus

HIV / AIDS

HIV / AIDS

remedi

medicine

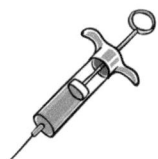

vacuna

vaccination

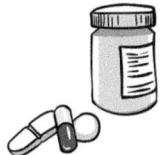

pilder

tablets

pilder

pill

yamada di emergencia

emergency call

aparato pa midi presion

blood pressure monitor

malo / saludabel

ill / healthy

auxilio!

Help!

alarma

alarm

atraco

assault

atake

attack

peliger

danger

salida di emergencia

emergency exit

candela

Fire!

brandspuit

fire extinguisher

desgracia

accident

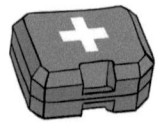

caha di prome asistencia

first-aid kit

SOS

SOS

polis

police

Europa

Europe

Noord America

North America

Sur America

South America

Africa

Africa

Asia

Asia

Australia

Australia

Oceano Atlantico

Atlantic

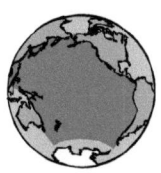

Oceano Pacifico

Pacific

Oceano Indio

Indian Ocean

Oceano Antartico

Antarctic Ocean

Oceano Artico

Arctic Ocean

Noordpool

North Pole

Zuidpool

South Pole

Antartica

Antarctica

mundo

Earth

tera

land

lama

sea

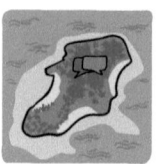

isla

island

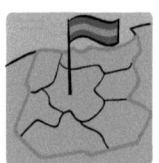

nacion

nation

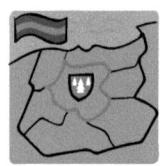

estado

state

holoshi analog

clock face

wijzer chikito

hour hand

wijzer grandi

minute hand

wijzer di seconde

second hand

Cuant'or tin?

What time is it?

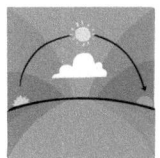

dia

day

tempo

time

awor

now

holoshi digital

digital watch

minuut

minute

ora

hour

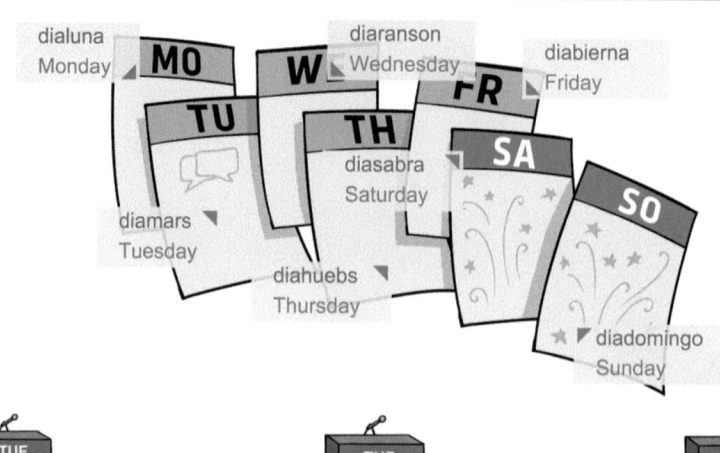

dialuna
Monday

diaranson
Wednesday

diabierna
Friday

diamars
Tuesday

diasabra
Saturday

diahuebs
Thursday

diadomingo
Sunday

ayera

yesterday

awe

today

mañan

tomorrow

mainta

morning

merdia

noon

anochi

evening

MO	TU	WE	TH	FR	SA	SU
1	2	3	4	5	6	7
8	9	10	11	12	13	14
15	16	17	18	19	20	21
22	23	24	25	26	27	28
29	30	31	1	2	3	4

dia di trabou

business days

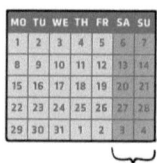

MO	TU	WE	TH	FR	SA	SU
1	2	3	4	5	6	7
8	9	10	11	12	13	14
15	16	17	18	19	20	21
22	23	24	25	26	27	28
29	30	31	1	2	3	4

weekend

weekend

aña

year

awacero
rain
arco iris
rainbow
sneeuw
snow
bientо
wind
lente
spring
herfst
autumn
zomer
summer
winter
winter

4.APRIL 11°
5.APRIL 4°
6.APRIL 13°
7.APRIL 8°
8.APRIL 10°

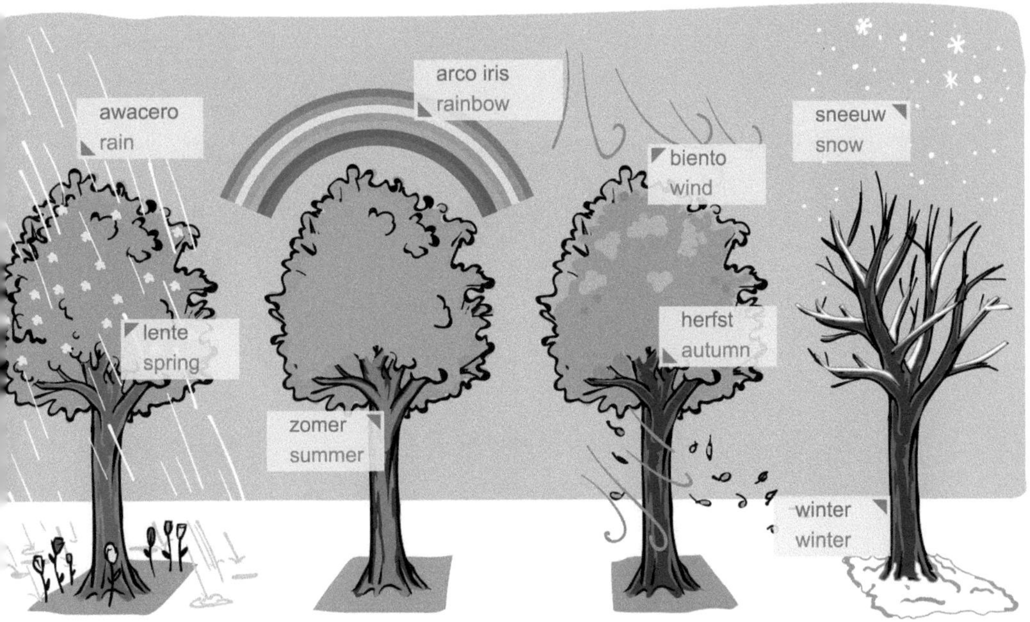

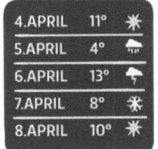

pronostico di tempo

weather forecast

F C
120 40
90 30
60 20
30 10
0 0
-30 -10
-20

thermometer

thermometer

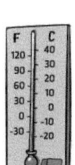

solo ta briya

sunshine

nubia

cloud

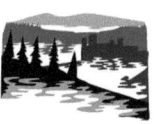

neblina

fog

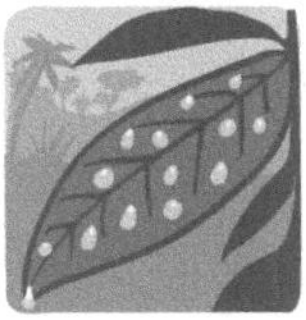

humedad

humidity

lamper

lightning

strena

thunder

mal tempo

storm

hagel

hail

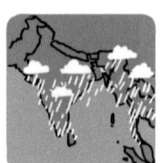

mal tempo

monsoon

inundacion

flood

ijs

ice

januari

January

februari

February

maart

March

april

April

mei

May

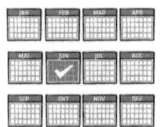

juni

June

juli

July

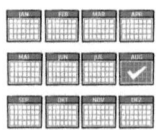

augustus

August

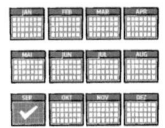

september
....
September

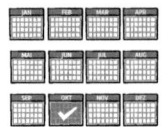

october
....
October

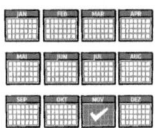

november
....
November

december
....
December

shapes

circulo
....
circle

cuadra
....
square

rectangulo
....
rectangle

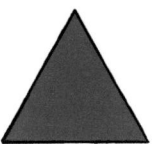

triangulo
....
triangle

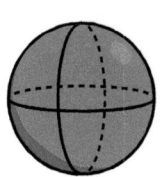

bol
....
sphere

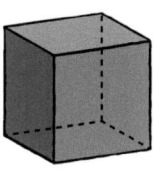

kubus
....
cube

blanco

white

geel

yellow

oraño

orange

ros

pink

cora

red

biña

purple

blauw

blue

berde

green

bruin

brown

shinishi

grey

preto

black

hopi / tiki

a lot / a little

rabia / trankil

angry / calm

bunita / mahos

beautiful / ugly

comienso / final

beginning / end

grandi / chikito

big / small

cla / scur

bright / dark

ruman homber / ruman muhe

brother / sister

limpi / sushi

clean / dirty

completo / incompleto

complete / incomplete

dia / anochi

day / night

morto / bibo

dead / alive

hancho / smal

wide / narrow

comibel / incomibel

edible / inedible

mal hende / bon hende

evil / kind

ansioso / ferfela bo mes

excited / bored

gordo / flaco

fat / thin

prome / ultimo

first / last

amigo / enemigo

friend / enemy

yen / bashi

full / empty

duro / moli

hard / soft

pisa / lihe

heavy / light

hamber / sed

hunger / thirst

malo / saludabel

ill / healthy

ilegal / legal

illegal / legal

inteligente / sabi

intelligent / stupid

robes / drechi

left / right

cerca / leu

near / far

nobo / uza

new / used

nada / algo

nothing / something

bieu / jong

old / young

cendi / paga

on / off

habri / cera

open / closed

keto / duro

quiet / loud

rico / pober

rich / poor

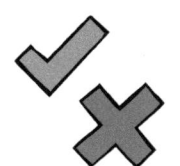

bon / fout

right / wrong

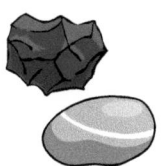

grof / liso

rough / smooth

tristo / contento

sad / happy

cortico / largo

short / long

pocopoco / lihe

slow / fast

muha / seco

wet / dry

cayente / friu

warm / cool

guera / paz

war / peace

0

cero

zero

1

un

one

2

dos

two

3

tres

three

4

cuater

four

5

cinco

five

6

seis

six

7

shete

seven

8

ocho

eight

9

nuebe

nine

10

dies

ten

11

diesun

eleven

12

diesdos

twelve

13

diestres

thirteen

14

diescuatro

fourteen

15

diescinco

fifteen

16

diesseis

sixteen

17

diesshete

seventeen

18

diesocho

eighteen

19

diesnuebe

nineteen

20

binti

twenty

100

shen

hundred

1.000

mil

thousand

1.000.000

miyon

million

Ingles

English

Ingles Mericano

American English

Chines Mandarin

Chinese Mandarin

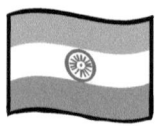

Hindi

Hindi

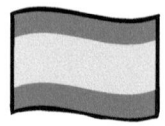

Spaño

Spanish

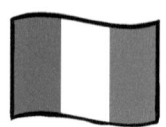

Frances

French

Arabe

Arabic

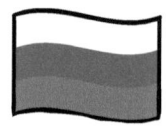

Ruso

Russian

Portugues

Portuguese

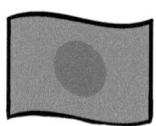

Bengal

Bengali

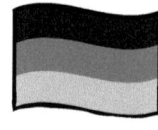

Aleman

German

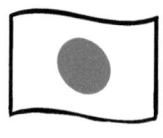

Hapones

Japanese

ami

I

abo

you

e

he / she / it

nos

we

boso

you

nan

they

ken?

who?

kico?

what?

con?

how?

unda?

where?

ki ora?

when?

nomber

name

where

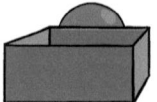

patras

behind

den

in

dilanti di

in front of

ariba

over

riba

on

bou di

under

banda di

beside

entre

between

luga

place